"**The most beautiful thing we can experience is the mysterious. It is the source of all true art and all science.**"

Albert Einstein (1879-1955)
Physicist. Wonderer. Not fond of a comb.

For Leo xx

I Wonder
first published in 2024
by Walker Books Australia Pty Ltd
Gadigal and Wangal Country
Locked Bag 22, Newtown
NSW 2042 Australia
www.walkerbooks.com.au

Walker Books Australia acknowledges the Traditional Owners of the country on which we work, the Gadigal and Wangal peoples of the Eora Nation, and recognises their continuing connection to the land, waters and culture. We pay our respect to their Elders past and present.

Text and illustrations © 2024 Phillip Bunting

The moral rights of the author/illustrator have been asserted.

 A catalogue record for this book is available from the National Library of Australia

ISBN: 978 1 760657 80 2

All rights reserved. No part of this publication may be reproduced, stored in a retrieval system, or transmitted in any form or by any means – electronic, mechanical, photocopying, recording or otherwise – without the prior written permission of the publisher.

The illustrations for this book were created digitally
Typeset in Apercu and French Fries
Printed and bound in China

10 9 8 7 6 5 4 3 2 1

Acknowledgement of country.
I acknowledge the traditional custodians of the land on which I live and work, and I pay respect to the Gubbi Gubbi nation. I pay respects to the Elders of the community and extend my recognition to their descendants.

I wonder.
PHILIP BUNTING

WALKER STUDIO

Have you ever wondered what we *don't* know?

Since the dawn of our curious kind, we humans have been quite fond of poking around at the edges of our understanding. We have gathered heaps of knowledge in doing so! Yet there is much, much more still to be understood…

I wonder what happened before the Big Bang?

Around 13.8 billion years ago, a single event pricked our universe into existence. We have a pretty good idea of what has been happening around here since the Big Bang ... but what happened before it? What caused it to go pop in the first place? What was *It*? Were there other universes before ours? Are there other universes out there now? We don't know.

I wonder what love is?

There are infinite ways to describe love, and it seems to be the answer to so many of our questions. But what is love, exactly? We know it when we feel it. Maybe love is why we're here? It might be that our finite hearts and minds will never be able to quite understand it. Perhaps there are some things that don't need to be understood.

I wonder if there is a god?

We humans idolise thousands of gods. Depending where (and when) you are, you might look up to Odin, Vishnu, Zeus, Thoth or Nabu. Our idols help us to make sense of our lives as we move through them. If there is a god, which one came first? And how did they get there?

I wonder what makes us want to be good?

We are a pretty social bunch. Humans live within groups of dozens, thousands, even millions of other people. These groups tend to work because most of us are doing the right thing, most of the time. But where do these species-deep impulses to get along come from? How do we instinctively know right from wrong?

I wonder what lies beneath?

We know more about the surface of Mars than we do about the deepest depths of the ocean. Never mind Martians, there are likely to be countless wild and wonderful forms of life we have yet to encounter, right here on Earth. What lies beneath? We don't know.

I wonder why we're here?

Is there some big plan – a universal reason for being? Many certainly believe there is. Maybe there is no reason. Or perhaps all meaning is unique to each individual. We don't quite know why we're here, but we can each find meaning through the people and things we love.

I wonder if we'll ever cure the −hic!− hiccups?

From the invention of the wheel to the World Wide Web, from −hic!− fishing to nuclear fission... technology has enabled us to do some wonderful things. Our innovation allows us to −hic!− see all the way back to just fractions of a −hic!− second after the creation of the universe. Yet, −hic!− alas, there is still no known −hic!− cure for the −hic!−hic!−hic!− hiccups. Argh!

I wonder what that's made of?

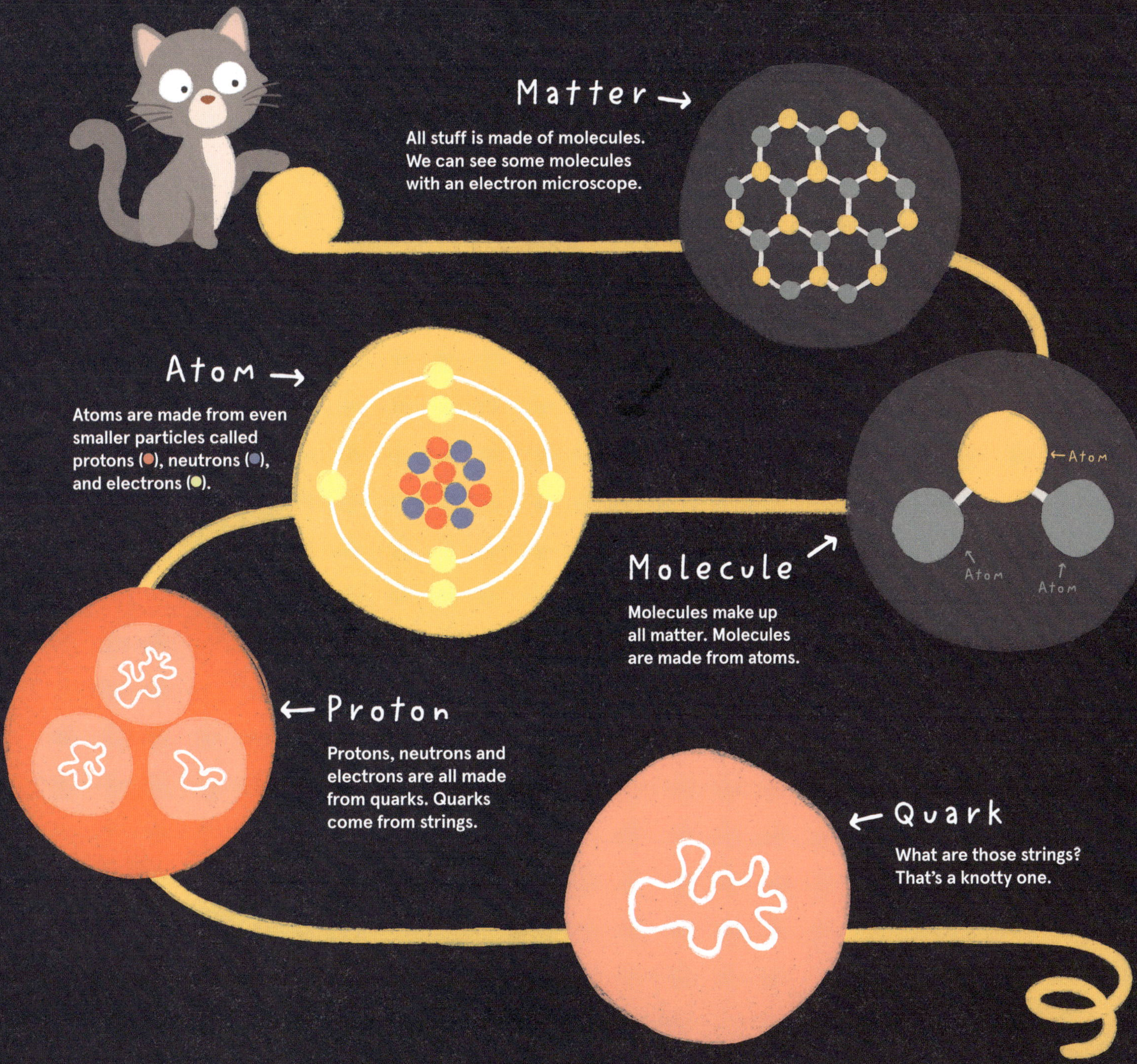

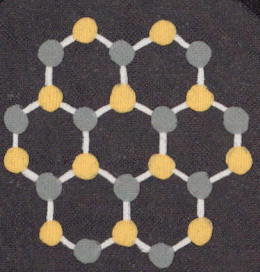

Matter →
All stuff is made of molecules. We can see some molecules with an electron microscope.

Atom →
Atoms are made from even smaller particles called protons (●), neutrons (●), and electrons (●).

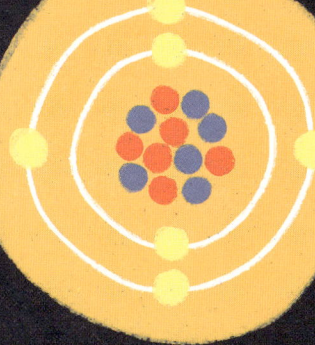

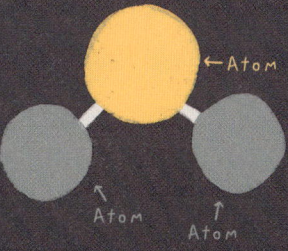

Molecule ↗
Molecules make up all matter. Molecules are made from atoms.

← Proton
Protons, neutrons and electrons are all made from quarks. Quarks come from strings.

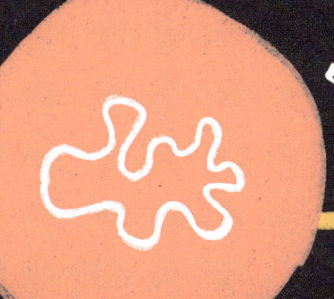

← Quark
What are those strings? That's a knotty one.

I wonder what we can not think?

In cahoots with our brilliant brains, our senses help us to picture the world through a lovely, manageable flow of thoughts. Just as a frame helps to focus our attention on a painting, our senses limit our thoughts about the world around us. Without these frames of perception, we'd experience an overwhelming flood of information. But what lies beyond our sensory edges?

Infrared

Many species of snake can sense infrared radiation. Thanks to their pit organ, they can create a thermal image of the world around them.

Magnetoreception

Honey bees are able to sense the Earth's magnetic field, thanks to teeny granules of iron in their abdomen. They use this super sense like an internal compass to navigate the world.

Echolocation

Most bats make little "clicks" then listen out for the echo. The echo of each "click" allows the bat to judge the position, size, shape and even the texture of the objects in front of it.

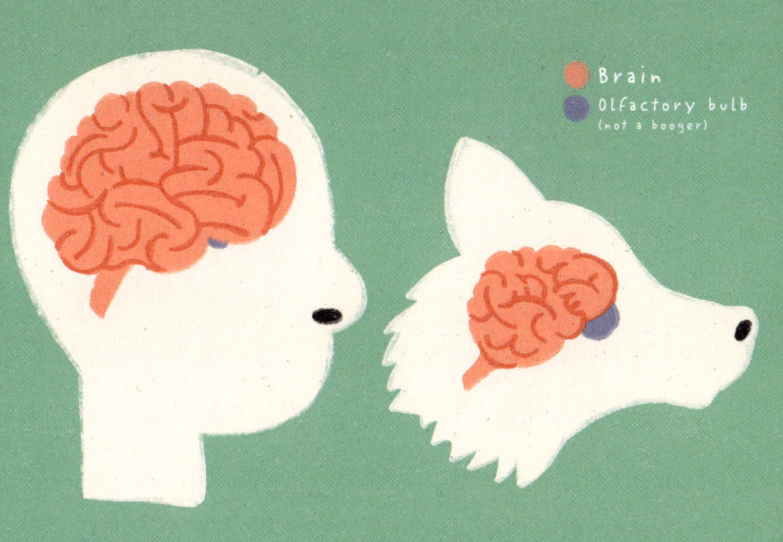

Brain
Olfactory bulb (not a booger)

6 million olfactory receptors

300 million olfactory receptors

Olfactory

With 50 times more scent receptors than us, dogs can create three-dimensional maps in their mind and even judge the passing of time through smell alone.

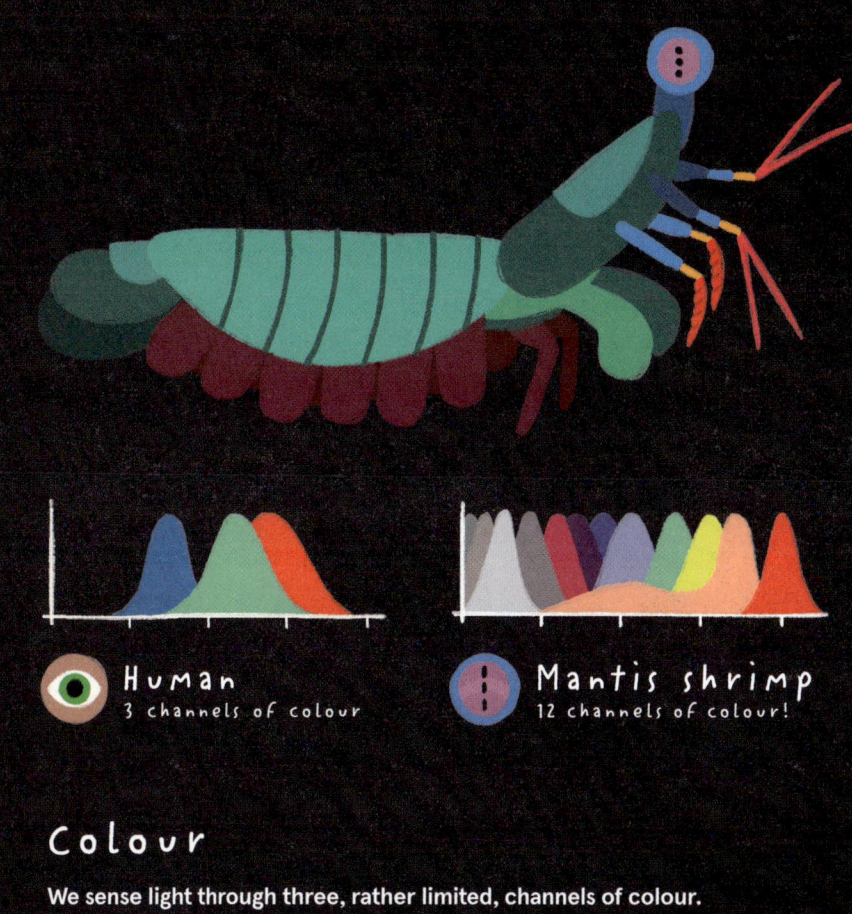

Human — 3 channels of colour

Mantis shrimp — 12 channels of colour!

Colour

We sense light through three, rather limited, channels of colour. The colourful, carnivorous crustaceans we know as mantis shrimps see the world through a tremendous 12 channels of colour!

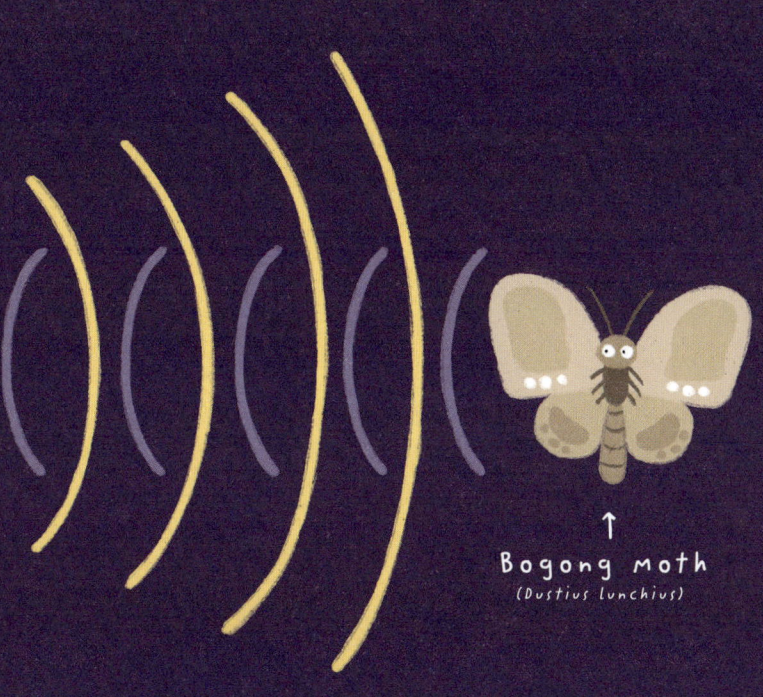

↑ Bogong moth
(Dustius lunchius)

Electroreception

Thanks to their super-sensitive bills, platypuses are able to detect tiny electrical fields emitted by living animals. This allows them to hunt in even the murkiest water.

I wonder what the universe is *really* made of?

We're pretty happy with our theories about what stuff is made from (molecules, atoms, protons, neutrons, electrons, quarks, and erm ... strings?). But matter only accounts for around 5% of the universe. The other 95% we know only as dark matter and dark energy. What are these things? We are still in the dark.

I wonder why I go for mint choc-chip?

When we make decisions, it feels like we're making logical and reasonable choices of our own free will. But are we really in control of the decisions we make? Some say our thoughts and actions are determined by things that have already happened. If that's true, your next big decision has already been made. Or maybe we do have free will, and you'll choose pistachio. *Eew*, pistachio!

I wonder why we need *so much* sleep?

We spend about one third of our lives asleep – which doesn't feel like a great use of our time here on Earth. Elephants get by on just two hours each night! But without sleep, our brains would not develop, our bodies would not recharge, our memories would fade, and our lives would be much, much shorter. But why do we need to spend quite so much of our time in bed? We don't really know.

I wonder if we'll ever go back?

We're all travelling through time at the same rate (precisely one second per second, here on Earth). But time is not quite as regular as that. For example, we know that time passes more slowly on the International Space Station than it does on Earth.* Is time travel possible? Theories suggest it is! But at this point in time, we really don't know.

*Not because they're bored.

I wonder why we cry when things get sad?

We hairy humans are the only animals known to cry when we're upset (or when we're really happy). Other creatures create the same salty solution, but only to keep their eyes rolling comfortably. So why do tears suddenly appear from the ducts around our eyes? Is it a literal cry for help? We don't really know.

I wonder if we see the same?

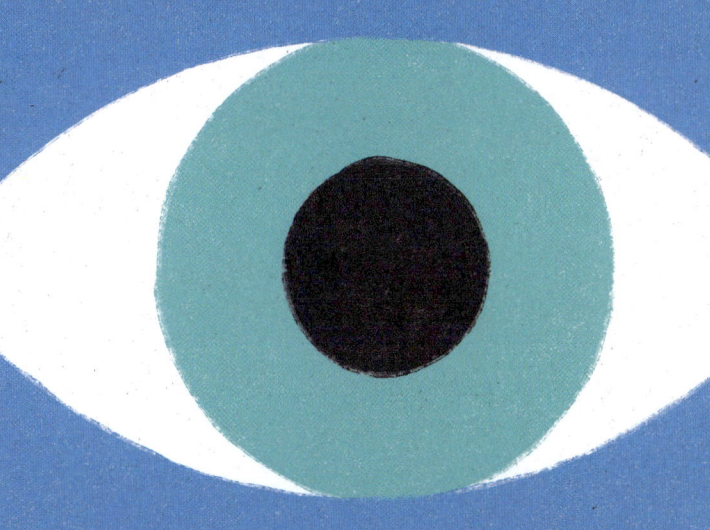

When you and I see this shade of blue, how do I know that it appears exactly the same to you? In your mind, this shade of blue might appear to be a little lighter, or more turquoise, or even the colour I call pink! How our perceptions form in our mind is entirely subjective (it's different for each of us), and none of us *really* know how others experience the world.

I wonder how life on Earth began?

A long while ago,* somewhere,** a bunch of non-living stuff combined to become a living thing.*** This first cell could make copies of itself, which – over billions of years – evolved into all forms of life on Earth. But how, *exactly*? Where? When? We don't know.

*3.7 billion years ago (roughly).   **In the ocean (probably).   ***Author's brain implodes (ouchy).

I wonder what makes me Me?

What we each think of as "Me" is really the result of lots of different processes happening in our brains and bodies, all at the same time. While we like to think of ourselves as a nice, neat, unchanging thing, we're really far more like an ongoing event – an ecosystem dependent upon other ecosystems. We exist thanks to the countless things that help to shape us. But if I take any of these things away, am I still Me?

I wonder how we wonder?

Every thought you've ever thunk came from your brilliant brain. But our brains are made from collections of unthinking atoms, arranged in just the right way for us to be aware that we're thinking at all. So how do our unique thoughts and experiences spring from a bunch of inanimate atoms arranged inside our boney bonces? We don't know.

I wonder if there's life out there?

 Our universe began with the Big Bang, 13.8 billion years ago. (Roughly.)

 Our life-giving star, the Sun, is 4.6 billion years old. (Or thereabouts.)

 The Earth formed around 4.5 billion years ago. (Close enough.)

 The first life appeared on Earth around 3.7 billion years ago. (It was a Tuesday.)

Ta-da!

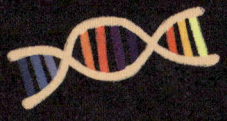 Which means it took less than 1 billion years for life to appear here on Earth.

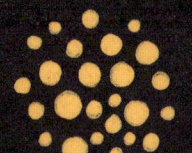 There are billions of trillions of suns out there, many of which are capable of supporting life-hosting planets.

 The chances of life having occurred around one of those suns, in the past 13.8 billion years, seem pretty good...

 But we haven't found any. Yet.

I wonder if a computer will learn to love?

Artificial intelligence (AI) can already do heaps, and may be the most significant human invention since Great Auntie[258] Wugga crafted the first wheel. But will AI ever become aware of itself, and then learn to love? It might soon be able to simulate self-awareness. However, there's something essentially non-computational about the things we call consciousness and love, and we still don't really know what that thing is. Perhaps the bots will solve that one for us…

Are we there yet?

I wonder what comes next?

A human lifetime plays out in around four to five thousand weeks (if we're lucky). Once our little show is over, the atoms that temporarily congregated to build our bodies are returned to the planet. But what of "Me"? Where does our awareness go? We still don't really know where it comes from, never mind where it goes. But wherever it was in the 13.8 billion years leading up to You, there's a fairly good chance the "I" in "You" is going straight back there, after this lifetime is up. One thing we do know is that our time on Earth is finite, which makes each moment ever more precious, and ever more beautiful.

Psst... There's no "I" in "You".

I wonder if this is all a dream?

Every now and then, life can feel too strange to be real. Some think our perception of reality is similar to a dream. Others believe that we exist only within a simulation, like characters in a really good video game. If this is a dream, I wonder whose dream it is? Whoever they are, I hope they're enjoying it.

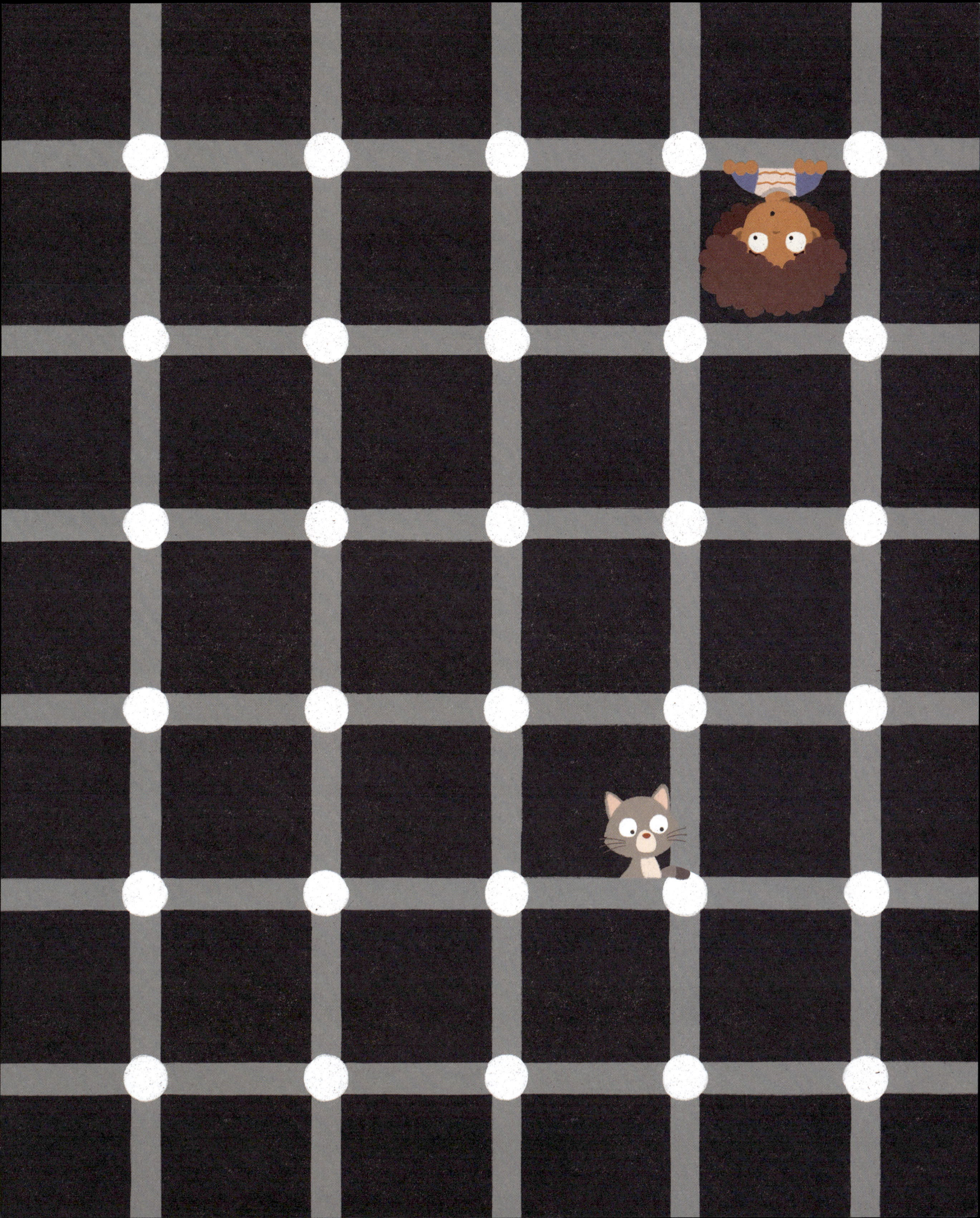